THE HIDDEN CHAPTERS

SOLA JOHN

DEDICATION

To my precious wife – Maybel Unyime John, whose eagle eyes spot the hidden chapter behind every trial we have ever been through. I love you dearly.

ENDORSEMENT

Hidden Chapters is a small but valuable resource material with inspiring and empowering stories and concepts. It is a dynamite that will explode greatness in every reader.

Congrats, John on this motivating piece.

Olumide Emmanuel
CEO Common Sense Group
Executive Director, Success Business and Leadership School
Senior Pastor, Calvary Bible Church and The Empowerment Assembly
Host – School of Money Seminars and Broadcasts

CONTENTS

ACKNOWLEDGMENTS

I give thanks to the Almighty God for giving me grace to offer this little to His people for blessings. My appreciation to Ugbede Paul Simon and Phillip Amiola for their editorial assistance. Also to Rev. Olumide Emmanuel and Pastor Segun Olugbemi for reading through the work and offering useful suggestions, I am grateful.

To my precious wife for her love and commitment to see me fulfill God's purpose. And to our children; Femi and Tope, who understood with me and gave up the playtime while I processed these thoughts.

Thank you Ayoola Arowolo, a beloved brother and partner in the ministry for your insights and perspective to issues.

And to Pastor Kennedy Olugbemi, my elder brother who took the pain to bring out God's gift in me. Sir, you are needed by every young man aiming at fulfilling purpose.

PREFACE

I COULD DIVIDE MY FEW YEARS ON earth to two phases. In the first phase I would say I served the devil with some degree of commitment. In phase two I came to know the Lord and served Him with absolute commitment. In all, I have come to a conclusion that nothing just happens.

There is a power that influences all we do. Often our will helps in enforcing whatever must have been concluded in the realm beyond us. But ultimately we can win continually if we realize that aligning our will with the positive will produce positive result no matter what the prevailing challenges are.

Winning always is not a wish but an option that can be made and realized. Our supposed failures and shortcomings are all working together an eternal purpose to release us into the ultimate victory Christ wrought for us on the cross of Calvary.

Thank you for accessing this little piece and may your thoughts be blessed as you digest these truths.

Olusola John
November 2013

1 STUCK IN THE BANK

HAVE YOU EVER EXPERIENCED an unnecessary delay when you needed an answer badly? It happens to us every day. A woman gave a testimony which has stayed glued in my memory to date…

She had made some purchases for her brother who was living overseas. In no time, the money was sent via money transfer. But it took her almost two weeks to get the money from the bank. She was disappointed and worried. She felt like a liar to the seller since she couldn't remit the money when she promised. She ranted at the bank manager and made several calls abroad to her brother for confirmation of necessary information. Eventually, she got the money and went to pay the business man.

That was when she learnt that the business man had been attacked by a band of robbers on the set date she was to pay the money! Unknown to her, while she was lamenting her woes, God was saving her from a dire situation by having her money stuck in the bank.

As simple as this testimony might seem, many people are still languishing in jail for offences they knew nothing about. They crossed the bridge at the wrong time and got into trouble. They were implicated in matters they were innocent. They thought they were on time but they walked right into trouble.

So when it seem things are beginning to delay beyond normal; your result is taking too much time to be prepared, your admission is not forthcoming…don't despair yet. Take another look. God is fighting a battle for you. All He is doing to preserve you from trouble is to have what you want stuck in the bank until Satan rides away.

That's true! For without our knowledge, God is fighting our battles for us every day. There are unseen forces in constant contention for our lives: the forces of good and forces of evil. They battle for our hearts, they clamour for our souls. We might not know because we cannot see them. But stack reality exists in unseen forces in the spiritual realm.

Once, a Reverend Minister asked God to open his eyes to see things happening around him. *'That I might just 'see' even for a second'* he cried to God. Then God let him. Oh gory scenes! He could not sleep for three days!

LESSON:

Ignorance can be good especially when the knowledge will not do you any good.

Do not be desperate on God because sometimes, the delay is for your own good. No wonder a wise man said 'in every situation, we must give thanks. Yes! Give thanks. When it seems the answer is not coming when we expect, give thanks.

When it seem time is passing you by, give thanks. Give thanks!

The answer will surely come. His hand is not short. It will come…at the right time it will come. Give thanks because to save you from trouble, God has stuck your answer in the bank!

2 MOVE ON WITH GOD

WE SHOULD NOT TAKE THE grace of God for granted. Although he holds us down so that danger can go ahead, we must be sensitive to know when he speaks.
Elijah left river Cherith when the water was dried up. He knew it was time to move and he moved! We need to know when God has moved so we can go along with him. It is very important as we go on in life.

God is our cover from rain and pestilence. He is our cover from all the arrows of the devil. In Him we live, in Him we move, in Him we have our being. We have to know when the cover of our soul has moved so that we do not unduly expose ourselves to the snare of the enemy.

Life is in stages my dear. It is like many bus stops on our way to a destination. Because a bus stop is beautiful does not mean it is your destination. Do not fall in love with the bus stops and forget your destination. You are not home yet until you're home.

All you need do is to act right and save time. There is nothing as important as an accurate sense of timing when following God. If He calls when the music is loudest then yield to Him. Whenever He calls just obey. Never wait beyond the right time.
This will help you avoid unnecessary pains. Though God is the same yesterday, today and forever He is so dynamic that when he is working in your life He does it with divine timing in perspective.

To everything there is a season, A time for every purpose under heaven (Ecc. 3:1). This divine timing is so important that if followed as led by the Spirit of God, you will avoid many traps and land safely in your destination.

There is nothing as important as the sense of timing in the New Testament believer. The terms of the new covenant in guidance is Sonship, Spirit led and Smart obedience. These will guarantee you a place and make you victorious. Delay can be dangerous.

When God moves on pack your stuff and follow. When He instructs you, don't wait for another second.

3 WHAT'S COOKING

THE BATTLE FOR THE SOUL and soil of Africa was finished at the Treaty of Tordesillas in June 1494 between Spain and Portugal long before they colonized the continent.

The plan to bomb strategic places in the US was drawn long before the actual manifestation 9/11. It took many years of planning and stratagem for Obama to make history as the first ever black American president.

Day and night, there were unseen meetings taking place in different places. The devil and his troupe strategize every day. God and his angels also strategize. And for what? For your sake! There are unseen battles going on man! The battle for your soul! That's how important you are.

The battle is so fierce that if our eyes are opened to see the tumultuous cacophony, we will be dumbstruck! But that's the reality. There is a battle raging on and sometimes we get caught in the middle. If not, why will a man like Job wake up only for calamities to befall him all round?

The truth remains that what we see *(physical)* are controlled by what we cannot see *(the spiritual)*. *Like* an aroma from your neighbour's delicious meal. It wafts through your nostrils. You cannot see the meal but you know there's something cooking! So the question is:

What's cooking? When you suddenly begin to experience a down slide in your life, what's cooking? When your container load of goods is suddenly seized at the port without any just cause, what's cooking? When you lost love ones in quick succession, what's cooking?

Like Job, is your faith on trial? Is someone trying to make you curse God and die? Is someone trying out his newly acquired atomic bomb at your back yard? What is cooking?

The devil hates your guts, man. He hates that you wake up everyday. He hates it but he cannot control it. He knows God has put a wedge around you and you're growing so fat in His protection. And sometimes we grow so fat we forget to pray. We grow so fat from God feeding us that we begin to feel we're doing it on our own. We want out. God is choking us and we need a fresh air.

At such times, when we are shaking up, we might lose our guard and fall out of favour by what we say or the choices we make. But if we are ever conscious of the love of God and like Job say, **'Though he slays me...'** we will remain steadfast no matter how the devil knocks us about. And the guy is a hell of a knocker! He knocks hard! See how he knocked Job…all kids gone! All livestock gone and a loose tongue wife to add salt to injury! **Curse God and die**. Day and night she persisted...*curse God! Curse God! Curse God!* Her persistent chatter alone could send a man into a fit.

But Job stayed on. He knows something is cooking and he trusted God to serve him a good meal at the end. And what a meal he got! Another set of seven children and lots and lots of goodies than he ever imagined. The bible recorded that God blessed the latter part of Job more than the former…

In this modern world, more than before, we need wisdom to perceive that God is really cooking something good for us; we need the wisdom of God for directions, not the chatter of the world telling us to curse God and die. And the chatter gets louder everyday; social media telling us there is no hope for the future, news of drowning world economy and a rising price in goods.

We hear the chatter that there is no hope for people living with HIV/AIDS and young people are doomed because the government of the day cannot provide job, Social and health security. When the chatters become unbearable, let us look unto God and say, *'abba Father, what's cooking?'* Constantly, God is working to bring His plans to pass in your life. He is positioning people, things and opportunities to meet your needs on a constant basis.

The hymn writer says; *"Christian seek not yet repose, cast your dream of ease away, you are in the midst of foes, watch and pray".* Nothing to fear and no need to worry, God is on your side and you are set for the top. The best way to maintain your peace is to know to whom you belong. Jesus said, we know we are of God despite the fact that the whole world lies in wickedness.

For whatever is born of God overcomes the world. And this is the victory that has overcome the world--our faith.
1 John 5:4.

4 HE IS A GOOD LAD, BUT...

A BOY ONCE ASKED HIS former school Principal for a recommendation letter. The good old Principal obliged and wrote   these words. 'He is a very intelligent boy. He accepts and carries out responsibilities and is academically promising but....'

As good as that recommendation letter might be at the first read, the cunning old Principal has planted a big question that will follow the young lad forever. *'But   what?' But he is a rogue?' 'But he does not come to work early?' But he is a murderer?' 'But he will run down the business?'* Well, of course we know this lad will never get anything from anybody.

It is like that in our lives. We hold a recommendation letter in our hands from our cunning old principal the devil. He knows our past and where we have been, he knows what we have done and how we have done it. He knows the people we have cheated, the girls we have gotten pregnant, the abortions we have committed, the lives we have snuff out…he knows them all.

And now we need a life from God. Here is our recommendation letter…'He is a good lad but…'   and we go with this letter gloomy. We are doomed! No one will give us anything with this letter. We are all directionless and we lost hope. How can we tender such letter before God?

We move about with low self esteem, wondering fare away from our future, running far away to where God cannot see us, because we are ashamed of our past, running far way from our destinies, groping in darkness.

We are overwhelmed with the weight of the 'but' that we fail to remember. We fail to remember the love of Calvary where Jesus washed everything away.

Okay he did take them upon himself but the guilt…why is the guilt still weighing me down, hitting at me from every side? Why does the devil still remember? If the devil remembers, then God remembers!

My dear, if you can just approach God with the letter in our hands, with all the 'buts' and all the imperfections, if we can just trust the finished work of Christ and move forward towards him, towards the plans he has for us…

I once carried a letter like that, full of 'buts', dark, dark 'buts' from my past that our Principal knew of. I took the letter and ran far, far way, to a place where I can hide my face in shame. For many years, I was still running. Like the Prodigal son, I stopped running one day. *'What the heck? Let what will happen, happen! I'm tired of groping in the dark, wallowing in self pity and self inflicted pains!'* Then I took the letter before God, trembling at what He will do to me if he sees my buts.

God collected the letter and studied it carefully. He looked up at me and back at the letter. My heart was trembling. What is He going to do now? As I was thinking, He picked His pen and scribbled something on the paper then gave it back to me. 'What is that?' I wondered. Did he write that I should be killed? An eye for an eye? That I should be cast away? My hands shook as I opened the letter...slowly, I opened the letter. The devil's statement was still there...*'He is a good lad but...Then I saw the new addition...'*HE IS MY SON!'

5 JUST AN ANGEL…

AFTER MY HIGH SCHOOL education, I had an opportunity to live with a family. My result was not good enough to earn me admission into the higher institution so I had to write my papers again the following year.

Along the line I had a problem with my host as I overstepped my bound to drive his car when I was sent on errand to call the mechanic. That resulted in a minor accident…the effect of the fallout led my young mind to contemplate joining the occult because of the frustrations and despair. Few weeks later events unfolded and I had to relocate to another state to live with another family.

Barely a month after, I had an unusual experience. The little congregation I attended had a special program for three days. It was during this period I surrendered my life to Christ. Eight years later while at the University, a classmate came to share his salvation experience with me. In an unusual encounter, God had told him how he must live as a disciple of Christ on the campus.

According to him, God showed me as an example of what He expects from him and then the young man began to tell me about my past. Wao! It was such an experience that I cannot forget. He told me how I had a crisis in my life after my mum's death which actually preceded the car issue I wrote earlier.

To cap the story, he said God told him how He sent just one angel to turn my face towards Him and ever since I have looked steadfastly at Him.

All we need in our lives to make an impact is just one angel…just one angel, turning our faces back to God, just one angel showing us the divine direction, just one angel guiding us to our great breakthrough. Just one angel!

It took just one angel for the greatest miracle of the world to happen. It took just one angel for Daniel's prayer to be answered. It took just one angel. And sometimes, angels do come in the form of men. Abraham unknowingly entertained angels in the form of three men and untied his miracle! We must be sensitive in the spirit so that we do not miss our angel when he or she passes by. In our work place, during recreation, when we pray or when we play, we must pay attention to what God is trying to tell us. Pay attention!!

Many of us have missed our replies to many years of prayers through sheer negligence. Our angel passed by in the form of a dirty old man seeking help, in the form of a young lad seeking direction, in the form of a young man who doesn't know how to use his ATM Card. But we just hissed at their follies and turn away our faces from them! We turn our faces away from our miracle.

How many times have we as a nation turned away from our angel who can lead the nation to greatness because he or she does not have the free money to throw around? May God help us all!

6 WINNING IN A GREATER WAY

ONE VERY IMPORTANT PART of a young person's life in Africa, especially Nigeria is to secure admission into the University, Polytechnic or College of Education.

Most time for us, the course doesn't really matter. What matters most is we are in the class of the *'elite'* group in the campuses. It was hell therefore, for a young lad to wait many years for admission. I was once in that hell.

When many of my mates were in higher institutions, I was still at home. My beards were sprouting all over my face. I was getting old! Still, JAMB *(the body moderating higher institution admission in Nigeria)* continued to JAM me. It was like they knew my face, as if anytime my photograph comes before them, they say, *'Ha! Customer again!'* as if they wanted me to continually purchase admission form.

The perspiration of desperation enveloped me and I wanted to get away, to a school, any school, and study a course, any course. Finally, my prayer was answered after three years! I got a pre-national diploma admission to study Estate Management in one of the Federal Polytechnics in my country. It was good news to me. I loved it because my dream of a greater tomorrow had begun. Though this program was to last nine months, it was better than remaining at home.

At school, I was very serious both in my academics and Christian life. I attended almost all Christian functions and led my departmental fellowship. God was working things out for me...so I thought until after my exams. When results were out I had failed a course. Anyone who attended a polytechnic in the Nigerian education system knows that when you fail a prerequisite course, it's goodbye to school.

The reparation of this failure was not lost on me. It meant I was leaving school...me, leader of fellowship, worker in God's vineyard, celebrated by friends and colleagues ... my friends especially my fellow Christians on campus were the more ashamed. They wept for me. They sympathized with me. They offered to help me out in any way they could. In all of these, I was unperturbed.

I kept encouraging them that things will turn out for my good. I could see a glorious future that they could not see. I knew what was unfolding was a big drama beyond my comprehension. I knew God was cooking something better for me. I knew I lost now so I could win in a greater way!

Not long after that, I secured admission to study Theatre Arts in a University. Many years have passed since then. I have learnt better ways to serve God with my talents and gifts. I have discovered that the reason I failed in the first place was that God had chosen me for a purpose and studying Estate management will not prepare me for that purpose. I failed so I could win in a greater way.

Yes! Winning in a greater way. We are all designed to win in a greater way so as to fill God's kingdom with heartwarming testimonies. Have you tried to find out why you failed that job interview? Have you tried to know why you could not graduate from school after many years of hard work? Have you tried to understand why God allowed those carry overs?

God wants you to win in a greater way.

He wants the devil to be put to shame in a greater way through the words of your testimonies.

7 GREAT GRACE

TINA WAS A POPULAR SEX worker. Children knew her. They could easily point her out to visitors.

One day however, her story changed. She encountered Christ and became born again. She got married later on, in the same neighborhood where she was known as a commercial sex worker.

Everything was perfect or so it would have been. But it was the beginning of her problems. Tina always looked back at the life she had lived and pondered on whether God had actually forgiven her. She would wonder if it was not all a dream, and if the bubble won't burst one day and her perfectly arranged life will come shattering over her face. Every time she wanted to move forward, the devil held the picture of her past before her. She became depressed. She became despondent. She became full of the idea that her past was too bad for her to be accepted by God.

Like Tina, many of us judge God by our human reasoning. We try to think for him, reason for him, measure his love by our human frailty. But the love of God surpasses all human understanding. He loves us so much that while we were yet sinners, Christ died for us. Such grace, such amazing grace! Oh, that Tina knows that the Grace of God had set her completely free! Oh, that she knows that all her iniquities He remembers no more.

God's grace had taken us from the filthy gutter where we once sat under the shackles of the devil, into the kingdom of his dear Son. His grace has given us the right to sonship, had catapulted us from swiveling pigs into riding kings.

The day Jesus died for us on the cross, the grace of God wiped clean our sins. He said boldly that our past, he remembers no more. When God said our sins are forgiven, they are forgiven. His grace is so overwhelming that even the host of heaven cannot understand why He loves us so much. Where Satan sees a condemned sinner, God sees a loving child. It doesn't matter what we have done. It doesn't matter the dirtiness of our past or the gravity of the offence. On the cross of Calvary many years ago, Christ had borne the iniquity of us all.

All we need do is enjoy the freedom of sonship. All we need do is recognize our place in God and embrace it.

As for the devil, he knows he is fighting a lost battle. The devil knows the importance of God's grace in your life so he'll do anything to keep you from enjoying it. That is why he keeps waving that picture before you.

Again I say to you, it's only a shadow of your past and Christ had dealt with it. You have a brighter future ahead of you. But the devil does not. Unlike you, he has a hellish future where he'll gnash his teeth forever.

So anytime he holds a picture of your past before you, hold a picture of his future before him! That'll hurt him real bad.

8 THE DEVIL AND HIS CHOICES

THE DEVIL IS FOND OF LOSING. Losing is his stock in trade. And it is because of a simple reason. He makes the wrong choices. In everything the devil had done, his choices had always been wrong and selfish.

It began when he tried to overthrow God. When this guy was leading the choir in heaven, he had a very sonorous voice coupled with beautiful appearance. That single mistake cost him his radiance and glory, pummeling him into a rather lightless world.

He made a choice to leave the presence of God rather than amend his selfish ways. And when he came into the world made for man, his presence here led him to trick the first man to selling his birthright.

For a while, he ruled the world made for man, dominating it and filling it with his vile; hatred, murder, premarital sex, incest and lots more. Then God decided it was time to give man back what rightly belonged to him. In came Jesus. Instead of the devil to calmly hand over the key to life, he made another wrong choice-he decided to put up a fight. First, he decided to embarrass Jesus.

Perhaps he thought the place of birth of Christ will determine His greatness so all the prestigious rooms were occupied and the only room left was in the manger. Again, he lost for Christ lowly birth made him the more relevant for he came to save the lowly and not the highly exalted.

When the Devil realized that Christ's lowly birth place was relevant for his purpose, he decided to kill him, another wrong choice. He began a search for the baby's head, killing every infant in the community.

Unknown to him, a word had gone ahead, **"Arise, take the young Child and His mother, flee to Egypt, and stay there until I bring you word; for Herod will seek the young Child to destroy Him."**

Guess what? When the devil troubles you too much God will keep your treasures under his nose until his last stumbling block becomes your stepping stone. The very child sought after was kept in Egypt. The headquarters of the tyrants of that time was Egypt.

The devil's wrong choice was motivated by his insistence to do things the way he like. Chasing after Christ, calling him all kinds of names (including the prince of devils) until he nailed him on the cross. He rejoiced in that for about three (3) days until there was heaven quake that brought Christ back to life. I call it heaven quake because earthquake swallow things from the earth but heaven-quake brought out the dead, raised Christ from the dead and changed human history. If he had known that sending Jesus into hades will cost him his hold on the keys to both life and death, he wouldn't have done it. But you know, he is fond of losing.

Now he is after you, a being fortified by the blood of Jesus. He throws bricks at you. He put tests before you. He put obstacles before your journey of life in order to make you fail. But if he had known that the bigger your test, the bigger your testimony, he would have let you alone. But again, he is the devil. He makes wrong choices and he is fond of losing.

Are your bills skyrocketing higher than your wages? Are you in a dilemma, lost on the next step to take? Are your kids getting out of control and giving you a fit? Are you thinking of throwing in the towel? Common friend, it's the devil we're talking about! Have you forgotten so soon? He never wins! He has never won anything in his life. He is fond of losing.

The devil's plan to bring you to this mess is one of his mistakes because you are coming out stronger. You must win. Your final victory is not negotiable. You are meant for the top. Your test carries your testimony. The bigger your test, the bigger your testimony.

The pain and pressure you have found yourself now is one of those stones that will take you to your high place. Even if he has dealt you a strong blow, he is not getting the final shout - you are. You will so flop him that he will cover his head in shame. Your lowest point is your lifting point.

Have you been let down? Don't worry you are about to spring higher than you have ever been.

You are that eagle in a story who has spent his life time eating with chickens. And then the chickens began to peck him so hard that he raised his eyes up into the horizon. He looked beyond the sun and his sharp eyes caught some birds flying. *'Hey!'* he thought to himself, *'I too can fly like that!'* So shaking his wings, he flew high, high, into the sky, beyond the sun until he was gone forever. Those pecks are to help you shake your wings. Shake your wings eagle and fly!

Flying is a choice you must make, dear friend. You must make the right choice. You must make that choice to take another look at your problems, no matter how big they seem to be. Take a better look at it and see a way through them for in every problem God has created a way.

So I urge you to take another look at your problems, no matter how big they seem to be. Take a better look at it and see a way through them for in every problem God has created a way. Make that choice now.

There is a story in the making of which a chapter is hidden from you. That is why you seem to be in suspense right now. That suspense is the hope you are exercising. You do not belong here. For he that is from above is above all. If you were meant to remain on the ground then I would have been worried but you are from above and above. More so, whatsoever is born of God overcomes the world. You are born of God and so all that concerns you.

The evil one has no power over anything that has to do with you. You are meant for the top so aim high for glory. If God permitted you to experience this, then greater story is coming.

For our light affliction, which is but for a moment, is working for us a far more exceeding and eternal weight of glory, while we do not look at the things which are seen, but at the things which are not seen. For the things which are seen are temporary, but the things which are not seen are eternal. 2Cor 4:17

Always remember that a book has many ends such as the end of a sentence, paragraph, chapter and page but the most important ending is the end of the last chapter. What chapter are you and why do you think it is all over?

Open the next page of your life...

9 WHY PEOPLE PERISH

LIVING AS THOUGH THERE IS nothing more to life is a tragedy of the ignorant soul which can lead to destruction. Hosea 4:6 captures it aptly that **"my people are destroyed for lack of knowledge: because thou hast rejected knowledge."**

Everyone involved in warfare must know his strength, the weapons available to him and the strength of his enemy. While the devil has been stripped of his power, he still has cunning devices. He offers false hope. He gives a picture of a world that does not exist. I remember a young man in the medical school who was deceived into drugs. 'It makes one feel high', he was told. Gradually he got involved until he wanted to walk in the sky. When his classmates knew something was wrong, it was late. Needless to say he could not complete his education.

Another young man was talented in playing acoustic guitar. He played to students who gave him stipends with which to pay his fees. One day my sister and her pastor visited me in the University departmental fellowship and the young man was playing to the admiration of everyone. My sister pleaded with the pastor to take over his sponsorship through the university. The good pastor agreed and I was sent to enquire about his academic work. We searched for him but he was nowhere to be found. He will never be found for he had been rushed home never to return to school because he suddenly went nuts. He had been on drugs and nobody knew.

He lost the angel sent to him too. Drugs offer a world that does not exist. Cultism offers power that indeed is powerless. Many tales abound of all the empty promises the devil gave to people that never came through. I was once by the death bed of a relative and he said to me: *"Satan has nothing to offer anyone. I have experienced all strata of life and if I have another chance of living, I will be an evangelist. There is no pleasure in sin."*

There is a new craze about the occult world in various dimensions. People want fame, power and money. They want to be at the spots where it is happening. Some mortgage their souls. While writing this book, I was driving past a bridge down town when I sighted a woman with a male assistant making incantations to a young lady dressed in white clothing with red stripes.

I wondered what she might be looking for but someone in the car offered an insight that she might be appeasing the gods for favor to secure visa. Bizarre as that might be, some mortgage anything to have their songs on top chart. For what profit is it to a man if he gains the whole world, and loses his own soul? Or what will a man give in exchange for his soul?

This lack of knowledge is the major reason why people perish.

10 TWO EXTREMES:
no devil anywhere and devil is everywhere

WH E N   I T   C O M E S   T O TALKING about our common enemy- the devil, there are two extremes people easily fall into.

One extreme is the belief there is no devil anywhere while the other says the devil is everywhere. Those who believe that the devil is everywhere are not right according to the scripture because he is a created being and has limitations. He was banished from heaven and he came down to the earth which means he is no more in heaven as you read this book.

When he came down to the earth, he had no place to live but he had to take over the serpent and deceived the woman. Ever since he was banished from heaven, Satan has remained a fugitive and still roaring looking for whom to devour. He seeks for an abode. Just as Christ said the Son of man has nowhere to lay His head, the place of abode He finally found was the heart of man that has become the temple of the Most High.

The devil desires a temple too and he won't even accept dwelling in trees or other mammals. The only attempt he made was when Christ chased him out of the tomb dwelling demon possessed man into the swine; the pigs revolted and ran into the sea where they all died. No animal has agreed to yield their bodies as dwelling place to the devil except the serpent. Satan is not everywhere. He can only be in one place at a time. He doesn't know everything. What you have not said he doesn't even know. He is not all knowing. Only God is the all knowing, all seeing and ever present.

On the other hand, to think the devil does not exist is not correct. Remember he was the archangel endowed with some supernatural powers and since the gifts and callings of God have no repentance; Lucifer lost his position but still manifests the angelic power God gave him. What gave us victory is the faith we have in the son of God that we are now sons. Since Christ became the first born among his brethren, we possess the power of sonship. For the Scripture says, **love has been perfected among us in this: that we may have boldness in the day of judgment; because as He is, so are we in this world**. We are just as Christ is with same power, authority, privilege and rights. God gave us all these that is why we may not have access to the

hidden chapters but we are sure of the end story.
   We won!

11 NO TO FATALISM

YOU SEE WE OFTEN ACCEPT things that come our way because we have become fatalists. That is what I call Christian fatalism.

From poverty to earthquake, some people think they are all acts of God. On the contrary I read that; **Every good gift and every perfect gift is from above, and comes down from the Father of lights, with whom there is no variation or shadow of turning**. (James 1:17)

God is not the author of evil. In whatever form it may come. Even if it comes under the most intense spiritual experience you have ever had, so long it is an evil experience; it can never originate from God. Do you know that no amount of test can reveal anything cat in the DNA of a dog? Just the same way you won't find evil in the DNA of God. Love is another name by which God is known. There is no evil in love. As a matter of fact, no fear in love, for perfect love casts out fear.

When things go wrong in your life don't ever think it is *an act of God*. He allows it for a reason. An example is the life of Job. God allowed the devil to test Job. But remember what he warned the devil? Job's life must not be touched. He allows it but he never approved of it. Children gone, livestock gone and a body full of sores with a nagging wife to add salt to injury. But at the end, God restored to him everything.

So when God allows pain in your life, he is sure to return a double fold blessing because though he allows it, he does not approve of it.

12 YOUR PERPETUAL TRIUMPH IN CHRIST

THE PERPETUAL TRIUMPH OF A child of God is not negotiable. It is your inalienable covenant right to be above all situations. He that is from above is above all. You have been raised with Christ, and seated with Him.

Sitting is a position of rest, hence, the apostle encourages that we strive to enter His rest. While men strive to work hard, you are exhorted to strive to enter into His rest.

The conviction you have can only be informed by your correct belief system in what God has done for us on the cross of Calvary. Through Christ's death, burial and resurrection, you are bound to be victorious by default. You are not permitted to be limited by circumstances and situations.

The day you believed in Christ, you were awarded three degrees; a B. A (Born Again) degree **(For God so loved the world that He gave His only begotten Son, that whoever believes in Him should not perish but have everlasting life** (John 3:16); an M. Sc (Master of Situations and Circumstances) degree **(Now thanks be to God who always leads us in triumph in Christ, and through us diffuses the fragrance of His knowledge in every place** (2 Cor. 2:14) and a Ph.D. (Doctor of Precious Promises) degree **(by which have been given to us exceedingly great and precious promises, that through these you may be partakers of the divine nature, having escaped the corruption that is in the world through lust** (2 Pet. 1:14)).

All these degrees were handed over to you on the day you got converted. Your victory is promised. You have precious promises which God made and since He cannot lie, and His words are so sure, then you are in for a great time. If you must be tired of anything, it is victory and if you can't be tired of victory you are up for continual success all round. Keep your eyes on Him as the author and finisher of the victory you enjoy. **And this is the victory that overcomes the world, even your faith.**

Read it. Believe it. Confess it. It is yours for the taking.

13 WHEN NEXT YOU FACE TRIALS

WHEN NEXT YOU FACE TRIALS and you don't know what to do, check what you believe. There is a strong relationship between what you believe and what you are experiencing right now.

While what you believe may either enslave you, God's thoughts will set you free. For the Word says you shall know the truth and the truth shall set you free.

When next you face trials, do not go about telling people what you are experiencing. Instead take your time to check your belief system. What do you really believe? Do you believe it is all over? Exclusive of your thoughts, check up what God says about you. What is His thought and plan for you? Has he given up on you? He will never! He has said He will neither leave nor forsake you. He is with you.

Then go to Him in sincere prayers and ask for just one thing- the revelation of Jesus. Let Him show you how precious you are to Him.

When next you face trials, do not ask for signs or miracles though they are good but they would not do the job. Can you remember Gideon? He asked for signs and still he was not easily convinced. When John was imprisoned, he sent a message to Christ to know if He was the one to come and Christ told the emissaries to relay all they had seen to John.

The significance of that according to Andrew Womack is that a word of prophecy had gone ahead in the Old Testament book of Isaiah. What John's emissaries saw was just a confirmation of what had been written.

Jesus is demonstrating to us that the most powerful tool of God for us at any point in life is the WORD. The word was made flesh to dwell among us.

When next you go through trial, if you must survive it, let the word be your anchor. Hold on to it as if your life depends on it.

Cling to it tightly and don't let go.

14 OF SIN, JUDGMENT AND CALAMITIES:
You are secured by the blood

THERE IS A WRONG CONCEPT of sin, sickness and calamities that suggests that when a believer is sick then it is as a result of a particular sin or when calamities befalls him then he has sinned. Some see it as God's judgment.

All these are not in line with God's word. A believer is a child of God redeemed by the blood of the lamb who was slain once for all for our sins **"For it is written cursed is anyone who hangs on the tree."**

The Holy Spirit convicts believers of righteousness, convicts the world of sin of unbelief and convict the devil of judgment because the prince of this world is judged.

Sickness cannot be from God. It is a lie of the devil which you must reject with all temerity. The Holy Spirit is there to tell you that you have been made righteous in Christ. This conviction will make you love God more and not feel condemned. Sickness is of the devil for the bible declared that all good and perfect gifts come from God.

Is sickness good? How about calamity? They belong to the devil so reject them. Now get this straight that all you are in for is a swell time with God. Christ came to give you life and in the abundance of it. Not sickness. Not death. Not poverty. Your security is the blood of the lamb.

When next the devil comes and shows you your past, show him the blood. That is his sign of defeat. He was finished by the blood.

15 ARE YOU FINISHED!
OR IT IS FINISHED?

EXPRESSIONS ARE VERY IMPORTANT to show what our impressions are. Rick Warren once wrote that impression without expression amounts to depression.

When the devil nailed Christ to the cross he said to himself *"I have finished him"* but Christ said **"it is finished"**! Here we are confronted with two finishing. One said I have finished him and another said it is finished.

It is important for you to understand this so as to choose where you belong. At every point of life you will experience challenges especially when it is time to make a new move.

You will keep stretching until you reach your ultimate goal of God's best for you perhaps at the sight of His face. When you are down and out or situations seems confusing. When you don't know what to do and everything seems bleak. And the ugly guy comes around to tell you *"hey guy, you are finished!"* I just got you there. Do you know how many people saw you messing up? Do you know how many have heard the story? Do you know you are finished? Do you know...? Do you...? Do...? Just tell him to hold on. Tell him you are not finished, rather, it is finished.

Tell the devil the story has been completed long before it started and you know the end that you won! Tell him you are familiar with victory more than defeat. You are in for victory. Tell him it is finished! Understand this as if your life depends on it because it is finished! IT IS FINISHED!

Christ in one of the most exciting moments said a profound word you must always remember: **"For the things concerning Me has an end."** (Lk. 22:37) Things concerning you have an end too. It must come to pass. You are on your way to testifying about the hidden chapters you will never read but the end of which you have seen. Keep winning. Give praise to God in your situation.

Shake off the depression. Take courage. Make your confession loud that you are not defeated. Praise God because you have won!

16 GOD IS FOR YOU

THEN GOD THE SUPREME CREATOR of all things saw how the devil deceived man to sign off his right to the planet, he worked out a permanent plan of buying it back.

Prior to then, the world has evolved a system of operation with Satan as the prince of the world. That system is a Babylonian system. It is a system that serves the devil's intent and purpose. The devil seeks worship in order to gain control and he in turn gives you whatever you desire.

He tried that with Jesus and failed. He asked him to offer worship in order to have the beautiful things of the world and Christ reminded him that man shall only worship God. The coming of Christ is to mark the end of the activities of the devil.

...For this purpose the Son of God was manifested, that he might destroy the works of the devil. 1John 3:8.

God loves you so much that he could give all he had to gain the world. He loved Solomon that he gave him wisdom and wealth but He loves you so much that gave all to have you rescued from the man who is bent on stealing, killing and destroying all you have. All these He did before you came to Christ. Once you are in Christ, he has your back. He watches over you. He neither sleeps nor slumbers.

He watches over you to ensure you are safe from the fiery darts of the evil one. He is your present help in trouble.

He said when you pass through the waters they will not overflow you. When you pass through the fire it will not burn you.

Keep winning! Keep celebrating the end of the story, is your victory!

ABOUT THE AUTHOR

SOLA JOHN is called of God to raise people that are passionate about God's Kingdom on earth. He is a Youth worker and teacher of the Word.

He is married to **Unyime** and they are blessed with children. They reside in Zaria, Kaduna, Nigeria.